Rainbow of a Dark Mind

By Al Baker

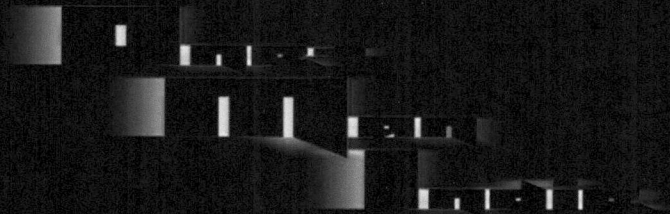

ISNB: 978-0-578-66971-7

Please direct all inquiries to:

One-Man Indie L.L.C.
PO Box 158
Forest City, PA, 18421
one-man_indie@outlook.com

Table of Contents

Dedications

To My Father, who read to me.
To My Mother, who inspired me.
To My Brothers, who walked with me.
To My Children, who amaze me.

To My Wife, who believed in me.

The Man That Never Was...

Is he real,
or just a dream?
Walks the world,
yet isn't seen.
By anyone.

He's the Man That Never was...

In the shadows,
he dwells.
Heaven-loved,
yet bound to Hell.
He walks alone.

He's the Man That Never was...

Oh, lost Son of Earth and Angel-friend.
When will you ever smile again?
Let the Sun arise and brighten your demesne.
Why cling to pain?

Although many things you'll see.
The whole earth you'll roam.
And of all the roads you trod,
Not one will lead home.
A sad and lonely destiny
keeps you wandering endlessly
Throughout eternity...

THERE IS NO BALM IN GILEAD.

I HEAR A SCREAM OF RAGING FROM THE ANGRY DEAD.
A STORM OF BLADED WORDS ARE RIPPING THROUGH MY HEAD.
A BLOODY ROAD, FULL OF DARKENED FANGS.
FROM BLIGHTED TREES, CHILDREN'S CORPSES HANG.

NO HEALING HANDS TO MEND...
NO SOOTHING SONGS TO LEND...
NO COMFORT IN THE END.

THERE IS NO BALM IN GILEAD.

THIS TANGLED DREAM OF MADNESS
HUNTS THROUGHOUT THE NIGHT.
WITH BURSTED WINGS, A BLOODY
EAGLE TAKING FLIGHT.
THE RIVERS SEETHE, WHILE THE
OCEAN BOILS.
A WEARY HEART BREAKS ON THE
SUN-SCORCHED SOIL.

NO HEALING HANDS TO MEND...
NO SOOTHING SONGS TO LEND...
NO COMFORT IN THE END.

THERE IS NO BALM IN GILEAD.

IS IT A PRAYER, IS IT A WISH,
OR JUST THE MUSINGS OF A FRACTURED MIND.
IS IT A SIGN, IS IT AN OMEN
TO FOREWARN US OF A FUTURE TIME.

...END OF THE LINE...

No HEALING HANDS TO MEND...
No SOOTHING SONGS TO LEND...
No HOPE AT ALL, MY FRIEND!

WHERE IS THE BALM OF GILEAD?

THERE IS NO BALM IN GILEAD!

Imprisoned

Forsaken in **Darkness**
Shunned by **the Light**
Endless despair surrounds me...

Bound by
Chains of the
Past

From flying
the Skies
of the
Future

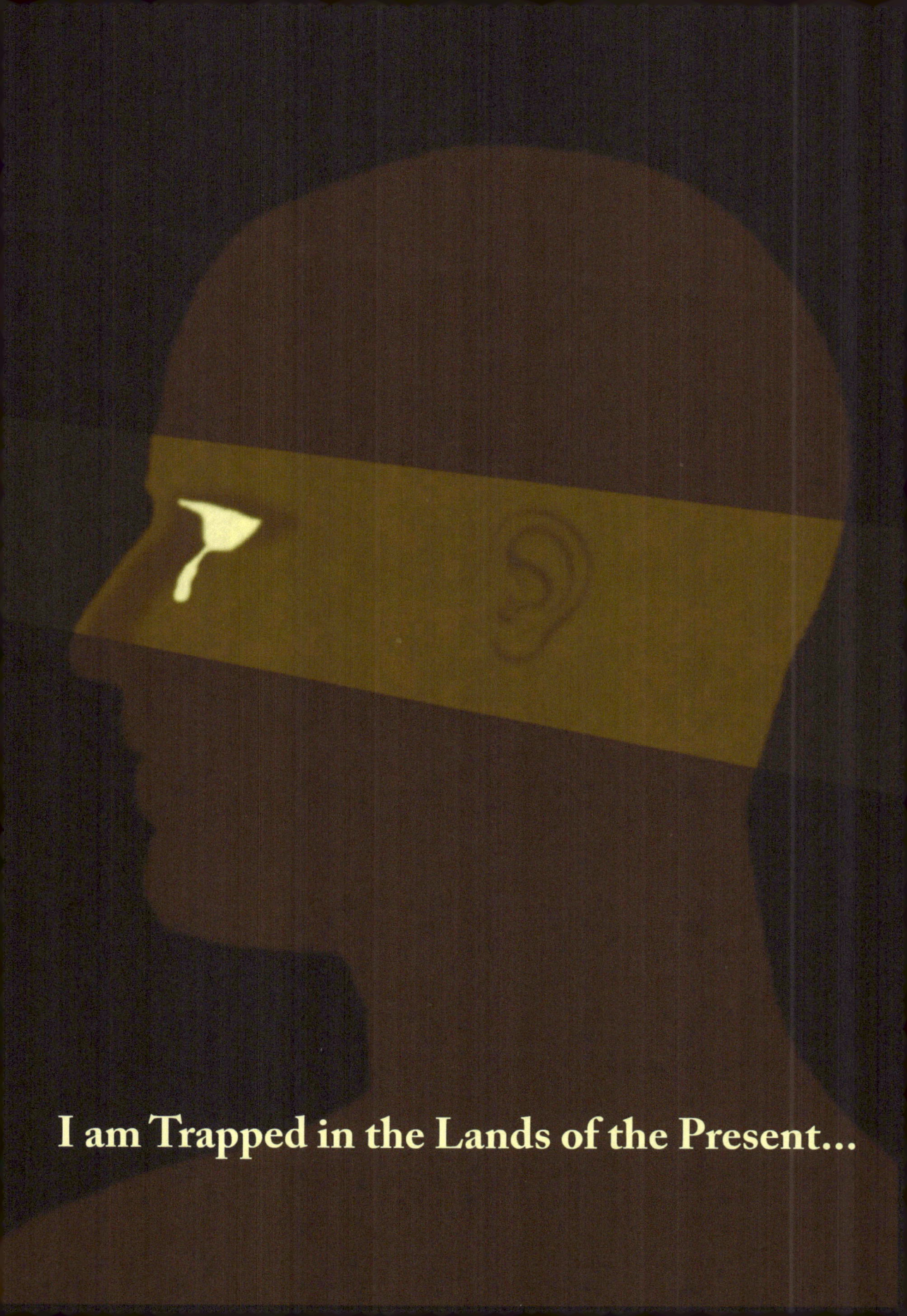

I am Trapped in the Lands of the Present...

Elegy of a Leaf

I hang at the edge,
seeing my inevitable descent
and accept it fully,
knowing I can do naught else.

As I begin my journey
to the world below,
I still feel a little fear
but I keep my faith.

Others, who have gone before
know this simple truth.
Life is an endless circle;
everything is connected.

As I finally come to rest,
laying with my siblings,

I await the Time of Renewal.

Death's Herald

My skill is keen—my blade is sharp!
To play Death's music like a harp.

I am the Watcher at The End.
To reap men's souls, so they descend.

I walk the Way of Wandering,
a dark and lonely route.
I view the Vine of Vengeance,
and taste its bitter fruit.

I dance the Dance of Desolation,
because I will spare none.
I sing the Song of Solitude,
for I am all alone.

In deepest reveries,
I see no kind Release.
Should EverNight embrace me,
shall I ever REST IN PEACE?

A Flower Blooms in Shadow

With heartbreak ever near,
a land laments.

In sadness
Living on seems trivial...

However, our purpose endures!

Indomitable spirits
see truth in love's languish.
For only understanding negates despair.

The Traveler

He walks in Darkness. From where, to where, is not known.

All he has known is traveling.

He longs to settle down and cease his drifting.

But Fate sweeps him up in an ever-rushing tide, pushing him always onward.

He hopes for a place where his roaming can end, to live his days in peace.

But he keeps wandering.

Until he comes to a place where he is safe; Permanent and Solid, A place he can call HOME.

Here the Lonely Traveler, the Weary Wanderer, can rest...

...and dream of Tomorrow.

A Word from the Author

Thank you for reading this work of mine. It
truly is a blessing to share my thoughts
and ideas with others. It's my sincerest hope
that you enjoyed the experience.

Strangely enough, all of the poems in this
book were written during different periods in
my life (teenager, young man, father).
Think you can tell which ones were from
which time period?

Scan the code below to join my newsletter and see my other products!